CRUSTY BITS OF
SCRAPPLE

Crusty Bits of Scrapple

SKETCHES, SCUFFLES AND TOUGH TALES FROM PHILLY

BY PAUL BUKOVEC

Paul Bukovec

IngramSpark

Intro/context

Grew up in the nineteen fifties melting pot hodgepodge of North Jersey. Ran the streets with a myriad of ethnic types. We were constantly teasing each other, and comparing nationalities and bragging rights about food, customs, and our respective religions.

In the apartment, my folks regaled us with stories of their first-generation experiences as outsiders learning the ways of the new country with parents from the old. Something about those tales and the emotional baggage carried within them left me fascinated by the marginalized. and the margins. Likely also contributed to my keen interest in narratives and how people tell them. I have always had a curious ear for accent, dialogue and idiom, coming from neighborhoods rich in a sonic variety of all the above.

Got a scholarship to a history-of-ideas liberal arts college program in New York in the nineteen sixties. Frightened and unready, I plunged head first into an immersive experience in western culture, beyond all expectation. After near drowning, I learned to swim. To float. To splash about.

Also got swept up in the wave of counter-culture/ anti-war activities. Became a resister, draft counselor, and a conscientious objector. Met a gal with wanderlust

and broader horizons who suggested that we do my
alternative service in a secondary school in Zambia. So I
went with her to Southern Africa, having hitherto been
hardly anywhere. And there a transformation began.
My color palette, musical taste, sense of culture, race,
and above all, xenophobia were all changed utterly.
Spent much of my free time engaged with students after
class, trading stories of customs, beliefs, values and
traditions. They taught me many things.

When I returned to the states I settled in Philadelphia
and chose a career path that would continue to satisfy
many of my curiosities and interests. Spent forty years
as a psycho-therapist in Philly. Began with a stint as a
mental health worker at Philadelphia State Hospital
while attending graduate school. I was then an
outpatient therapist at a Mental Health Center in the
Far Northeast, at that time one of the whitest
neighborhoods in Philadelphia. After that, I taught at
Temple University for five years while conducting a
small private practice in the Germantown neighborhood.
Saw a clientele consisting mostly of thirty-something
New-Lefties and low-income political organizers.

I then began a three-decade period designing,
supervising and serving as the lead clinician for the first
ever treatment program for domestic violence/abuse
perpetrators in Philly. Tough work. Requiring a tough

approach. Built a diverse staff: male/female, pro-feminist, gay/straight, black/white. Assembled several crews of hard-nosed clinicians to run a safety-first, accountability focused counseling center. It was engrossing work. Felt important. As life changing for the staff as the clients. Both heady and humbling. Reflecting back, I feel gratitude for the privilege. Fortunate for the opportunities this work provided.

I was privy to intimacies, customs, street culture, and language far beyond my own experience. As a second generation, up-from-the-working class, white man, I got to engage in vivid interactions with men from backgrounds very different from my own. I had thousands and thousands of hours of deeply intimate conversation with African American men, with immigrants from scores of countries, and with white men from every ethnicity and social class. Spoke to their wives and partners. I hung out with drug dealers, teachers, tradesmen, clergy, factory workers, health workers, doctors and techies. They broadened my perspectives and my world view. It was exhilarating. Rewarding. And exhausting. I am left with a swirl of memories. Lots of characters stand out. So many random details. So many dark tales. Triumphs. Failures. Bizarre twists. Moments of quirky humanity. Mundane profundities.

This is a collection of portraits, sketches, and stories that are pieced together from those memories. Most of the characters in this collection are mosaics. Constructions from fragments, shards and wisps of recollections of people I encountered in my work. Most of the narratives are fictional, but also true. As in, they were constructed, in large part, from details actually reported to me by individuals. I have, in some cases woven and interspersed random pieces into new characters and stories. I have also made some stuff up. It is also true. To their stories.

And the pieces can be a bit grim. Some contain a touch of humor, a hint of irony, and/or my own version of Slavic cynicism: one that retains a streak of stubborn optimism. My characters are sometimes presented in their own personal idioms. They exist in my head as they presented themselves to me. They came to me within a very unique context. I share them with you from that context.

Also, by way of explanation, I got a paper cut on my mind reading The Day of the Locusts back in college. The subsequent infection and fever left me with a darkened sensibility.

Contents

Leroy

COMING UP HARD

Leroy was raised up
in Alabama with his grand-people.
Saw his momma seldom.
Acted like his older sister
when she did come round.

Grandma was the sort
who read her bible
home on Sundays.
Treated Leroy fair
but had him cut
his own switch if he was bad,
and he had better bring
her something with some heft
or there was hell to pay.

Granddaddy was a quiet man
with a streak of mean when
crossed. Sharecropper.
Kept a knife
in his boot he could

1

throw true and
swing precise to slice
a man in a fix.
Taught Leroy
to handle the slingblade he
gave him on his fourteenth
birthday. Showed him how
to palm the shank flat
and flip it out and open
in a snake-arm strike
up and across.

That was the move that
forced young Leroy's
migration north to Philadelphia
after he cut two bucks outside
a speakeasy in town when
he had just turned eighteen. Was
likely time to move on, anyways.
But Leroy had to make fast
tracks and never got to say
goodbye to his grandma.
She died the following year.

Leroy was a man-child
so big boned he could pass for
thirty, long as he kept to
hisself and didn't act too country.
Did some shaping-up down
at the food distribution center
till they got to know how good he
worked. After that they picked him

regular. Got a furnished room,
a fedora, and some fancy shirts
to wear on weekends. Steered clear
of the slick dudes. Mostly drank
his little gin by hisself or with
a dark-skinned older lady down
the block who eyed him friendly
coming from the corner store.
She had big teeth,
a wide bottom, laughed real
hard, and got down to business
sweet after peeling shrimps on
Friday night. Her teens were older.
Never got in the way, so it was good
for a time. Till one day at the Chinese
take out, some doo-ragged fool
wants to stand in Leroy's way coming
out the store. Must a been high
or just too stupid not to show basic
respect to a man who carried hisself
like he might be holding something.

Which, of course, dude found out, sliced
from hip to rib and gushing like a stuck pig.
Eighty-seven stitches for the corner
bull. Leroy got eight years with time off
for keeping to hisself, which came natural.

Joe

(LOVE AT FIRST SIGHT)

"How'd I meet my wife?

Well... I was workin' for
this loanshark
in Kensington
who sends me to this bar
to tell the owner he's
got till the end of the week
to pay up before somebody
comes back to make
him walk funny.
Crowded place, with a dancer
in a cage on the bar
and lots of regulars drinkin'
and singin' and shit –
so I walk up to the guy –
deliver the news –
and he gets pissed and wants
to send his own message
on my ass back to my boss
- proceeds to try to fuck me up-

but I got two back up soldiers
and we commence to fight our way
to the door – breakin shit
and throwin hands and
shoving people out our way...
and I happen to look
up and catch the eye
of the stripper in the cage
– and she smiles at me
– and I smile back –
and I think to myself
I'm coming back for you!
And I did.
We're married now
goin on twelve years.

That's how...

Vicky

Child of Fishtown

I

Vicky's mom loved pushing her in the stroller
window shopping on the avenue. also loved
chewing the fat in lawn chairs on the stoop
summer nights till swarming to the tap room
neon light with neighbor ladies thirsty for a cold one.

after working at the factory, Vicky's dad loved
dancing darlin daughter round the kitchen while
mom finished supper dishes. also loved tossing back
a few brews with the guys after dinner down the bar.

mostly they'd both wind up watching their Phillies
or their Flyers together with the gang at the corner.

their row home sat cross the street catty cornered
to the fire station. some nights screaming sirens
roused small Vicky from her sleep. trucks rippin
and roarin. dogs howling round the way.

they'd find her wet and frantic clutching the rail

of her crib when they stumbled in 'bout eleven.
usually it took a while to settle her down
till they all fell asleep together.

II

one St. Paddy's when Vicky was bout six they
cleared the first floor to make one long row
of card tables end to end. small coolers for beer.
plastic bowls for chips and pretzels.

Vicky watched neighbors hauling nips and pints
and jug wine for the ladies. they sang Irish
songs. drank laughed and drank lots more.
rowdy harmonizing all the night.

Vicky joined other kids swiping sips from cups
till dad ruined everybody's fun throwing punches
at Mr. Ryan for flirting with her mom.

in the melee Vicky got cut on a broken pitcher.
eight stitches at St. Chris'. dad never did come home
from the precinct. never had another party at the house.

III

Vicky got knocked up first time she had sex.
night of junior prom. round her way they
giggled bout an expensive wedding...
pearl handled shot guns...

smart as a whip. nuns said she was college

material though they didn't mention where
the money would come from.

Timmy was a piece of work, a few years older,
hunky, horny, and stubborn as a cinder block.
always with a brew in hand talking shit.

thin-skinned-know-it-all deserving
of a good swift kick. or, better yet,
Vicky's mom would say, a good beat down.
which he never got but did hand Vickie
every now and again behind nasty hang overs.

just before the second child was due Tim
went off bout some nonsense. punched
and choked her bad. down to her last
nerve Vicky took out a restraining order.
filed charges. went back to mom's.

Tim took a deal to avoid jail time enlisting
in the service which those days meant
an all-expense paid trip to Nam. Vicky was
guilty/grateful when he didn't make it back.

waitressed at the tap room till old enough
to work the bar. poured drinks; grandma babysat
the boys. cute as a button. still with her figure.
lots of tips and admiration from the owner.

after Timmy, Tony seemed so much more mature.
the older man approached politely like how Vicky
imagined a gentleman would. they were soon

at it hot and heavy after work till sure enough,
she's got another bun the oven.

but on account of the fact that Tony was long
married with grown kids and a wife on chemo
Vicky had to go. picked up a shift at the diner
till baby girl was almost due. Tony helped with
incidentals: pampers and the like. up to when
he threw a stroke behind the bar and passed
away. never sick a day in his life.

IV

heart bruised and gun shy Vicky stayed
single quite a while. focused on the kids
and slinging diner hash. had regular
good tippers lining up for breakfast
wisecracks smiles and that "what can I
offer you, hon?" that left some grown
men tingling with ideas. that's when
Ron caught her fancy not cause he
tried so hard but cause he didn't.

Ron wore quiet confidence. a warm smile,
and nice dress shirts to his office
at a corner table in the diner. business card
said insurance agent. in truth he was a bookie.

stood out from Fishtown guys with his pinky ring
and a gentle manner. also the only man she'd
ever met in her entire life who golfed. seemed
an interesting kind of odd. exotic almost.

the flirtation took forever. Vicky lingered
mornings at Ron's table ribbing his high
falutin ways teasing him for bigger tips. he
played it cool, slow rolling his eyes, shaking
his head at her zingers, leaving folded bills
beneath the plate. finally asked her on a dinner
date to Jersey where Vicky had only ever
been on a few trips down the shore.

kept company through a brutal winter.
saw him almost all the time. Vicky's mom
was charmed. the children liked him too.
everything was copacetic till springtime
came and Vicky found herself second fiddle
to Ron's first and favorite love: the greens.
played two rounds each both weekend days.
sometimes wednesdays too. Vicky's fuse
began to smolder. had her fill of being
a distant next in line. everybody said
she was lucky to find a guy who'd tolerate
her situation: saddled with a bunch of kids.
and here's a guy with a few bucks in his pocket.
owner of a nice car and a decent disposition.

"thank your stars" came the unsolicited
suggestion: "take the bad with the good."
another piece of sage advice. which only
served to piss her off the more.

Vicky couldn't shake the gnawing hurt. or
the melancholy. also in the mix: a

yearning to be a special someone she could
dimly recall yet never quite remember.

folks were shocked the day she kicked
Ron to the curb in spite of being pregnant
with her fourth. held her head high.
no regrets she would admit. glad to have him
visit his daughter when golf schedules permitted.
in no need of further heart ache from this or any man
who wouldn't or couldn't make her number one.

V

at thirty nine with four kids and hot flashes
Vicky says she's ready for the change.
even if it's coming early. probably shoulda
tied those tubes stead of listening to the priest.

not that she doesn't love her kids. god
bless em. but enough is just plenty enough.

not that she's lookin much for romance
nowadays either. enjoying being on her own
hanging out on the stoop with lady friends.
keeping up with the kids' school work.
visiting that program at the center.

lately she stares hard in the mirror
rehearsing warm accepting looks
at the plump but pretty face that
stares back grateful to be cherished
like a favorite child.

Dominic

(Tangled up in Blue)

Dominic was a beat cop
who got jammed up
during a domestic.
But not on the job.

Dom grabbed his wife's face
so hard she called 911.
Marks still on Angie's cheeks
when the cruiser arrived.

Responding officer
tried to do
Dominic a solid.
Had him take
a walk to cool down.
Wrote it up
for him to skate.

Dom's conscience
wouldn't let him.
Called a program.

Ashamed and guilty,
unloading to a stranger.

At home, Angie could only
surmise; wild with suspicions…
he wasn't giving anything up.

Brooding. Tight-lipped.
Couldn't admit there was
somebody else,
or the more humiliating truth:
the other woman was gone;
ditched his ass completely.

Strung out on longing,
Hating himself for it.

Even more pathetic than
the original sin of falling
for his on-the-job partner:
now he had to watch her
wide-eyed for another cop.

Station house gossips whispering
like old women. Some asshole leaving
marshmallows on his squad car seat.

Always thought himself a cut above.
Never hung out in cop dive bars.
Didn't let easy broads, crazy for
the uniform, turn his head.
Family man; father of three. Not

a whore like so many of his peers.
Not until he drank her in
over coffees in their parked
unmarked. Not until the haunting
bits left him craving:
rushed unbuttonings,
grabbings from behind,
furtive fucks,
the smell on his fingers;
the funk on her lips…

Rode up on a robbery-in-progress
with his head so far up his ass,
he left his weapon in his holster.
Walked into the bodega like he
was looking for a quart of milk.

If the perp is on the scene,
Dom's a dead man.
Instead, just another thing
to kick himself about.

Sad dumb fuck.
Dangerous at home.
A menace on the job.

Still pining for someone
who couldn't care less.

Marriage hanging by a thread.
Supervisor breathing down his neck.

The kicker?
He would gladly
throw it all
away for her
again.

In a broken-heart-beat.

If he only could.

Joel

Clearing the Bases

it comes to him
in a flash.

an epiphany
while stirring
coffee.

mid motion.
nearly spins him
off his chair.

the too often
laundered sheets.
that oilstain
on the driveway.
those bruises
on her back.
the lingering wisps
of room deodorizer
hanging suspended
like her

nervousness.

incongruous
made coherent.

he fumes
mind revving.
but tagging up
before racing
home.

takes a little time
to formulate the plan.
but not much.

next morning
he leaves home
as usual.
drives a few blocks.
stashes his car.

walks back
to the house.
waits round back
till Lisa leaves
for exercise class.

goes in.
changes
into sweats.
grabs a bat.

lies down
tight against
the wall
under
the fourposter.

coiled amidst
the dust bunnies,
Joel lays
obsessing:

a glowing
hot pustule
of swelling
humiliation
replaying
slo-mo
clips.
rerunning
hints and clues.

incriminating shreds.
missed bits.
oblivious
naive moments.

the montage
is interrupted
by Lisa's noisy
return.
the thud
of her gym bag.

footfalls to the fridge.
loud gulps.
she flips on the stereo:
Chrissie Hynde.
The Pretenders.

Joel seethes
clenched
in a cloud
of dry ice
steam.

dude arrives
soon thereafter.
they go right at it.
feral animals.

wild scuffling.
heavy panting.
grappling
in the foyer
banging
into things.

in the doorway
to the bedroom
frantic wrestling
out of clothes.
one body falls
onto the bed.
then the other.
grunting.

sighs.

"OH YES! YES! OH YES!"

Joel close
against the wall
in frozen fury.
nauseous.
rage
expanding.

then
he is
suddenly
standing.
quivering.
bat cocked
above
his head.

a voice
erupts
in a roar
from
almost
outside.
behind.

louder
than he's ever
screamed.
but alien...

as
from
beyond:

"YOU
FUCKING
SCUMBAG!!!"

the first blow
lands flush
against
the man's
back.

the second
grazes
his head,
cracks onto
his shoulder.

"MOTHERFUCKER!"

Lisa is screaming

"OH NO! OH NO!
OH, PLEASE NO!
JOEL, PLEASE NO!"

all at once
just as randomly
as the tornado
sucked him up

it drops him down.

drained.
bloodless.

he hears
a hoarse
whisper
as from a
ventriloquist's
tight lips

"get the fuck out."

then with a sharper edge,

"Both of you..."

mad silent movie
scramble.
anxious darting eyes.

herky jerky.
farcical dashing.
grabbing at
bits of clothing.
throwing on and
stepping into.

all askew
they leave
the door ajar.

drive off
in separate cars.

Joel stands
bat across chest
taking in
the keystone
cop retreat.

snorts
a bitter
laugh.

flips the bat.

sits down
and weeps.

Kiki's Heart

Unlucky in Love

In her late forties Kiki was still
hoping to find herself
a solid guy. pining for a keeper.

her standards weren't super high.

a man with education.
decent job. his own car.
not too many children.

or lots of baby moms.

did her time in the dance clubs
in her twenties and thirties.
went out in a posse of friends.

had her little fun.

a few odd boyfriends along
the way. couple of longer term
flings. nothing that lasted.

or landed her a ring.

aged into oldies night "parties"
thursday evenings. had her
share of hoots. boppin 'n slidin

bit of jitterbuggin...

after while got to feeling
like those early club scenes.
only now, the gents were older.

set in their ways.

confirmed bachelors: man
caves, fancy grills,
pimped out bedrooms.

mirrors and dark walls.

her folks had wanted the best
for her. so she was one
of those Catholic school Baptists.

one of three black kids in her class.

East Mount Airy born; mom, secretary,
dad, worked the post office.
nice row home on Upsal St. big yard.

aspiring to bougie not reaching for Jack and Jill*

her Catholic college scholarship
in Scranton went unused
when she chose Temple.

closer to home and homies.

pledged Zeta Phi Beta.
lifelong sisterhoods. studied social
work. got her MSW on a a free-ride.

DHS paid her to work and go to school.

slow to pick up on the musical chairs vibe
around the few available men in the department.
never got her butt down fast enough.

good dudes snatched up quick.

finally took momma's advice.
went back to church. joined the choir.
sang alto in the middle row. noticed

the choir master smiling at her a lot.

got to talking after practice. went for coffee.
hit it off. he had a way of telling stories.
gesticulating dramatic like a maestro.

laughed deeply. beautiful smile.

the courtship, a whirlwind. fast and

furious. making up for lost time.
modest of means. church mouse poor.

but well dressed, extravagantly mannered.

unencumbered by kids, debts or alimony.
seemed an answer to her prayers.
until she heard whispers from the back pews.

dream boat might just be the perfect nightmare.

church ladies knew the word: gospel,
verse and tasty tidbits. choir master
indeed a gem, but, alas, a costume jewel.

in robes and in the closet: the man was on the down-low.

so ended Kiki's turn to Jesus. gave up singing,
even in the shower. returned his friendship ring.
the mark on her finger washed away eventually.

the pain in her heart lingered.

*Jack and Jill of America is a leadership organization formed during the Great Depression. African American mothers founded it in 1938 with the intention of bringing kids together in a social and cultural setting. It is headquartered in Washington, D.C. *Wikipedia*

Tony

Closure

Wild assed tree climber
couldn't/wouldn't sit still.
Maybe speeding on caffeine;
maybe scared.
Could be hypomanic,
or all of the above.
Pacing the office
in Carhartt overall cutoffs
and a sleeveless tank top
oblivious to the irony
of wearing a wife-beater
to his intake for
a domestic violence
evaluation.

Hair screaming out the
sides of his head;
beefy arms full of ink
pumping punctuation
for his motor-mouth
ramble-on.

I ask him to tell
me about his tattoos
thinking it might
chill him down.
Sure enough,
he pulls up a chair
and begins the tour:

skips over the dragon, the tiger
and the tribal graphics:
"this here's for my daughter,"
(a cherub with her belly
emblazoned Chrissy)
"that there is my son,"
(a furled banner
with the name Anthony).
"Here's my wife, "
(A big heart with a filigreed CANDY).

"This here
was my first wife, "
he says fingering
a raw red raised
rectangular scar
on his left bicep.
"Took her off
with a belt sander
after she left me."

Lola

Taut String

her translucent skin and dandelion
hair produce their own aura.
illuminate the room.

but in repose, she usually
appears not quite still.
verging on skittish.
impermanently poised:
dragon fly just alit.
flight risk any moment.

in chat, the caffeinated
cadence of her banter
can surprise.

far less delicate than first
impressions might suggest. edgy.
staccato phrasing, eyes darting
to punctuate each sentence.

not at ease. not at all.

a blurter. strong views.
mostly unsolicited.

minimally burdened
by information
beyond her personal
experience. Lola is yet
possessed of many opinions
to expound on. drop of a hat.

decades ago, a runaway from
a small town near Athens, Georgia,
Lola, in late teens stumbled pregnant
from the Greyhound to a waitress job
on Passyunk Ave. made her way
with guts and grit and looks that
opened doors. long as she smiled.
and spoke sparingly
in her lovely quick-step drawl.

got a tiny flat near the market.
took up with an old black dude
round her way who did odd jobs.
seemed kind and wise. sold rolled
joints as a side hustle.

he was un-fazed
by her chatter.
smiled his stoner smile.
shook his hoary head
as she ran on bout silly stuff.

was tickled at the looks they
drew weaving through weekend
crowds on 9th & Christian
browsing vendors at the market,
she with big belly, he workin
his shabby ace-of-spades-strut.

some hard core I-tals mumbled
shit about their race and age.
Lola appeared to gloat.
old dude to sneer
spitting squirts between
front teeth to shine his
I-should-give-two-fucks
veneer.

supported her through
labor and recovery.
never blinked when baby
turned out mixed
through no fault or
contribution of his own.

grew tighter. more settled
over time. domestically tranquil
cepting for her endless chatter
behind her ever-constant worries.

those anxieties took
an unexpected upward spiral
one warm summer night
when old dude threw an embolism

as Lola gave him head with intense
attention to precise detail.

bereft, embarrassed,
humiliated, AND abandoned,

Lola curled into a ball.
hid out. scraped barely by
for quite a while desperately
blinking her mind's eye
at the macabre memory
of herself some kind of
femme fatale mantis.
dear old Chalky consumed
in ecstasy. gone in a spasm.
bitter swallow. coitus terminus.

the hamster ran its wheel
at breakneck speed inside her head.

Lola fretted through tortured
hibernation months on end
till finally forcing her nervous energy
into forward gear: got herself
subsidized daycare, secretarial school.
then a nine-to-fiver and fresh digs
up in Germantown, where there were
fewer questions and cheaper cribs.

unsurprisingly, Lola kept a no-profile
on the dating scene burdened
by a stigma only she was privy to.

still drew attention from dudes lured
by her exotic look. but Lola stayed
aloof. threw herself into motherhood;
obsessive foraging of health food,
crystals, essential oils, and natural
dyes and fibers.

hemmed some pretty wraps. wove scarves.
knitted mittens in her spare time.

soon hawked her wares at craft fairs
and flea markets weekends.
started hanging out with artisans,
artists, and a few musicians. eventually
caught sight of a rambunctiously
dedicated young jazz drummer
who practiced feverishly in a row home
on the back street behind her building.

went round one morning to ask if he
could start his routine a wee bit later
in the AM. had playful banter bout
his chops, devotion to his music and her
need to get more sleep to face her day.

one thing led to the next.

Lola got swept up by his energy, flirtatious
eyes, beautiful dreads and quick strong hands.

but she was mostly captured

by his straight-ahead style:
few preliminaries. little foreplay.

passionate kisses, rushed caresses,
clothes pulled askew: found his rhythm
quick, hard and steady. down to business
first and every gig: right up till the climax.

so it came to pass that Lola got to enjoy
a little lust again. get past the morbid
memory of sucking life out of old dude
and was released by the thrill of young
dude making funky music with her. not
that she was freed of any of her other
buzzing harpies. but at least that one
major fury had finally relented.

the fling with young dude was short lived.
ended pleasantly enough. Lola fretted only
briefly. then nervously got back to the frenetic
business of making her own way. she remains
there still. perched vigilant, almost ready.

Jack

Walk on the Wilde Side

"I'll jump off that bridge when I come to it"

Jack was a bisexual part-time transvestite
on the down low. a half-stepping addict
in quasi-remission when they met
at the dog park. Jill was a recovering
alcoholic burnt out from years of fag hag
pining for guys who couldn't love her
"that way". she'd sworn off the life
given up the bars and made friends
with friends of Bill W when she saw Jack
with his Airedale. she recognized
him from the rooms. wasn't sure if
she'd seen him at that meeting
in the gayborhood though. she had
an Airedale too. Jack wasn't sure Jill
looked familiar. on the way for coffee
their leashes crisscrossed impossibly
on the sidewalk. they soon were entangled
also. razor wit. arcane AA aphorisms. that edgy

queeny schtick that so often drew her
into impossibly painful crushes. alarms sounded.

she tried backing away. he pursued. she slowed.
he put some fervent moves on. she was delighted.
grateful. and surprised by how good he was
with his tongue. Jill also noticed that he flipped
to finish her from behind both those first times.

but she was having so much fun she let it pass:
entwined in a swirl of wrassling. passionate
chess matches. bouts of cribbage. dueling dishes
of stir-fried veggies. wild fucking on rumpled
sheets. and so much staying over it made more
sense for him to just move in.

Jack confessed to intermittent switch hitting
but pledged to bat from only her side
of the plate from there on in. then he
fessed up to the occasional predilection
for satin underthings electrolysis, and
queen anne pumps. sirens tripped. scabs
got ripped; but she was having so much fun,
she let it go.

Jack's urge gradually emerged; edging
to a pang; sharpening to a craving; itching
to be satisfied with exact rituals and
precise ceremonies. she watched in morbid
fascination and swelling dread.

two lines of speed set his edge aglow

from tingle to throbbing insistence.
a couple of long hits of bud before
browsing through the closet boxes:
perfect threads to spread across the bed.
another hit. the steamy bath. the safety
razor. the full-length slather of shaving gel.

"Nothing quite so sexy as that raw feeling
after shaving from your eyeballs to the tops
of your feet" he beamed. she wobbled.
scared but titillated. intoxicated in the spell
of the metamorphosis. another toot of meth.

the ensemble; matching shoes; the preening;
the rehearsing; she helped him with his makeup
like they were best girlfriends.
"ready on the set, Miss Desmond,"
she whispered, excited to the edge of fright.

they ventured forth for girls' night out:
Shirley Temples at an anonymous bar.
well and good, and kinda fun till they
started catching eyes and free drinks
from bar-flies looking for a hook-up,
or a hand-job in the alley.

Jack's neck flushed. goosebumps.
Jill's stomach boiled. bile. she tried
to squelch the burn with rapid appletinis;
her face ablaze; her program aflame.
she became enraged.

their brawl cascaded into the street.
she cursed him all the way home.
threw his shit to the pavement. Jack
begged. swore he'd never cheat
or go out in drag again. but this
time the yellow lights flashed red.

Jill recalled a brilliant junkie she
met in rehab years ago.
when confronted with the question of
what would become of all his high flung
plans when all his playing with matches
finally burned him, he scoffed:
"I'll jump off that bridge when I come to it"

"been there; done that!" thought Jill,
surveying the wreckage.
she yelled, "time to leap!"
she slammed the door.

Jack didn't quite get the reference.
but he knew what she meant.

Jimmy

Unfit

Jimmy owned a few workout centers.
Self-made entrepreneurial fitness guru
by day. Miserable pop-off by night.
Outbursts. Wild accusations. Threats.

Had a dark side not even his wife
could fathom. No idea what
was eating him. Or where all
the wild shit was coming from.

Jimmy wasn't exactly sure either.
But he had a hunch he tried not
to pay attention to.

Wrestling back in high school,
Jimmy made weight bundled up
in steam rooms and hiding out
in toilets: enemas and vomiting.

He was crazy for the hand-to-hand,
the grappling and the take downs.

Got herpes on his face grinding
heads with other boys on the mats.

Took his love for combat to the army
where he was shocked to wash
out of Ranger training school
for fighting with the wrong sergeant.

Found himself a civilian gym rat.
Soon in cahoots with a meth huffing
ex-Navy SEAL down in Delaware.

They pumped with white lines
and mad reps screaming challenges
in each others faces,
overloading muscle groups
and falling into exhausted hugs.

The SEAL dude convinced him
to join in on a spree of late night
stick ups at random gas stations
and convenience stores. Stocking
masks and sawed off shotguns.

The crystal whipped the rush
and drove them to distracted
paranoid suspiciousness of almost
everything. Especially each other.

One night Jimmy woke up
to the SEAL barking behind
a flash light beam and a rifle

barrel staring him in the face:
"ARE YOU READY TO DIE?"

Jimmy talked him down. Made bacon,
eggs and coffee. Took the car out
for cigarettes. Jumped on 95.
Never went back.

Laid low in Philly. Kept his head down
for a while before beginning a gradual
ascent from trainer, to supplement salesman,
to spa manager, all the way to fitness tycoon.

Hired a cutely anorexic exercise
instructor to do step work and spinning
for the ladies. Soon they were
grinding each other into exhaustion
and hastily wedded bliss. But only
until Jimmy began to come undone.

Bits of memories started arriving
unannounced. Clips and scenes
intruding in flashes startled him by day.
Phantasms jacked him upright in the night.

Fragments. Incriminating apparitions,
insinuating innuendo testifying against
everything he had built, represented
and become. Weird urges, crazy thoughts,
emerged from god-knows-where.

Spooked and panicked, Jimmy flailed

wildly searching for a goat to blame.
She was available. He lashed out
at minor irritations. Short fused.

Resentful even of her chirpy disposition.
Started accusing her of veiled
contempt and submerged hostility.
He soon had earned both.

Eric

Baby Momma Drama

First babymom was in ninth grade.
Left school behind it, though he wasn't
going much anyways. Caught his first case
a year later. Dumb shit. Boosting a GPS
from a Chrysler. The bigger fuck-up was
fighting the policeman who caught him
red-handed. Juvie time at St. Gabes.

"Loved dat joint. Hooked up with some solid
dudes. Played some football. Learned a little
something at the school too." A first for him.
Out before he turned 18. Back in the street
without missing a beat.

Delivered a little product here and there.
Tried some retail theft with a crew at the mall.
Gave that shit up after barely out-running
a rent-a-cop and missing his ride back
to the city. Then got two girls pregnant
a month apart. Shit-storm of drama behind
that: Screaming and yelling. Yanking each other's

extensions out in the gutter. Scratches all up
and down his back trying to separate them.

Tried staying with one of them;
then the other. "Just had to bounce".
Too many questions. Too much in his face.

The worst was yet to come: Shamika.
Older than the others. Seemed a welcome
bit of strange. Had a nice place. Teen kids.
Cable. Did hair in her kitchen. Always extra
cash on hand for beer and take-out.

That honeymoon did not last. She got pregnant.
Demanding and moody. First time he went AWOL,
she exploded. Swears he should of quit her then,
but he hung on for a few more nights, hoping
to catch the big fight on HBO.

Serious mistake. Scrolled his cell while he was
in the shower. Hit him with a skillet upside
his wet nappy head. All kinds of shit jumped off from
there: Horrendous scuffle. Neighbors call the cops.

Catches two counts for assault. One for reckless
endangerment. While he's inside, Shamika tosses
out all his shit. Had to go back to his mom's
and to a program. Plus, he missed the bout on cable.

Harry

Christmas Dispirited

Lizard skinned,
bug-eyed,
bony faced reptile
of a man
once a carpenter
now a crack head
on probation
for assaulting
his sadly simple
poor-soul
of a wife-in-recovery.

Ordinarily
we'd assume
he's lying
if his lips
were moving...

Today he bullshits
his check-in
at the treatment group

saying everything
is copacetic at home
and all with the missus
is cool too.

Meanwhile
she just called
to say he went
on a tirade
about her moving his stash
and threw
the Christmas Tree
out the window
late last night ...
how her heart is broken
this being
her favorite holiday
and he knew
damn well that
it would crush her.

We ask him to sit
outside in the hall
till he can come clean.
He keeps walking.

She's not there
when he gets home.

Away in a shelter
dreaming about Magi...

Lamont

Meteorite

He dropped out when the cash, bling,
and easy pussy made school seem like
a waste of time. In the street, he got
props for his connections further up the chain,
but dudes from other crews gave that teeth
spitting cold stare they do. That same
"you-ain't-shit" glare the cops deliver
from patrol car windows rolling slowly by.
Despite the drama, and all the looking
over his shoulder, things were pretty good
for a minute: money for his moms and
baby mom, cool shoes, bad ass rims,
a crazy snake collection in the bedroom,
and the finest chronic for his posse.

A coupla years of drive-bys, sweeps,
county jail time, and a hard-assed P.O.
forced Lamont to look for safer gigs
to bring in bread. Only dead end, low
wage bullshit: flipping burgers; detailing cars.
Nothing delivered cash like the corners could.

Shorty wasn't happy neither. Spoiled
by all the high life. Zero left over
from the days of Hennessy and lobster.
Now that the flash car was gone
to pay for pampers, now Lamont was
her Buster: A scrub who had to call his best bull
to drive his shit back to his mother's
after Shorty had the police kick him out.

Then she copped an attitude when he passed
by to see Little Man and Chantel.
Always with her hand in his pocket,
sweating him for more.

Boiled over one night, when he popped
round her crib unexpectedly and found
an old-head gangster from round the way
up in her spot playing with the babies
trying to get next to her. Had to leave out quick
to avoid a thing with old dude and his bunch.

Lamont rolled up on Shorty next day
in the street to have a word. That jawn
went bad from the jump: Disrespect.
Calling him out his name: Punks and bitches
and pussies. And shoves. Lamont clocks her good.
Next thing he knows, he's got a cop's knee
on his back, getting cuffed on the pavement. Almost
had to go back inside to finish his bit, but instead got a
deal for a program and more probation.

Ernie

First Born Son

Ernie grew up fast and hard in Tacony.
misbegotten family. the only Jews for miles.

mom, the local crazy lady.
dad, the guy who vanished to Jersey
after a furious screaming match
with his ranting wife.

left behind to watch his brother's back and
listen to the inconsolably weeping madwoman
stumble through the chaos of the wrecked apartment,
Ernie learned lesson one in the street:
the more shit you take now
the worse it gets next time.

mastered the art of getting off first.

sucker punch or quick kick
to catch would-be tormentors off guard:
at the hint of taunt, or sneer or whisper
about their whacked mom, their ratty clothes,

or the crusty bits on their unwashed faces,
he'd come out swinging.

randomly pissed at all comers. head on full swivel.

eleven-year-old banger whose only peace
was time at school where oddly he thrived.
where teachers gave him wide berth.
let him have his moods if he kept them to himself.

smart kid. loved to read. and swipe candy
from the corner store. and binge on chocolate
with his brother in the bunk bed with the lights out.
three years of bedlam, forged report cards,
running streets, candy stealing, fighting
all comers, Ernie comes home from school
one day to cops carting off his mother.
302 commitment. State Hospital.

held his brother's hand in Family Court
bracing for foster care, till dad
miraculously appears through the side door.

judge assigns him custody.

now thirteen, Ernie toes a different line. on a tighter ship.
each night the old man returns from work.
fixes a crude meal. asks a few questions at dinner.
Ernie washes. his brother dries. dad reads till
slumping into a crumple of newspaper
and armchair upholstery in the pale tv glow.
skulks off to bed.

Ernie pinches a few bucks at a time. buys random
paperbacks, a pocket knife, Hershey Bars. and cans
of beer from Georgie Wynn round the corner whose
brother steals them out the back of the beer distributor.

drinks alone late at night. squirts the warm foam
in his mouth catching suds inside ballooning cheeks
then swallowing fast into a dizzy buzz.

less family face to defend. less brawling. still an edge.
now a few kids round the way to hang with.
silent props. respectful distance.
space for the big boy who goes off.

which he doesn't as much now.
instead bulks up with Joey Ippoletto's
dumbbells in the basement storage bin.
power lifting. pecs and lats. pecs and lats.

no school sports no cliques.
no clubs. just obsessive power lifting
pecs and lats and stacks of random novels.
holds his no-pressure spot atop the B group class.
gifted underachiever. gets a little grocery store job.
pocket cash. six packs no longer hidden from his dad.

in Golden Gloves he boxes too hot.
caught by a jab, he rages. can't keep
his chin down or hands up...gets pasted
by a punk who sticks to fundamentals.

stumbles into a dojo up on the avenue
looking for a kung fu movie. finds a sensei
strangely calm and steady.

learns a different way to breathe. stand correctly.
find his balance. or try. cause that part proves
to be the hardest. always.

first Sunday every month they ride the boulevard
to the end. visit Esther in the asylum. watch her
eat a box lunch like a pogrom refugee.
listen to her rave non-stop Armageddon.

Ernie looks a lot like Esther. has her coloring as well.
people say he's her spitting image. Ernie hocks
a phlegm-thick loogie whenever he even blinks at
what that could mean. but deep down he's just sad.

she is too possessed to recollect the sweet times.
moments that flood Ernie suddenly: the smush
of her breast in hugs; "Ernie, Ernie" in his ear;
the tang of borscht; aroma of chuck roast brisket;
the quiet sizzle of latkes; that distinct smell
of goodnight cold cream… back when.
before her mind got lost in a cloud of furies.

Ernie loves the old sensei. hangs at the dojo
whenever. also loves his beer. keeps these
infatuations separate till the martial artist
notices something's in the way.

Ernie lies. cannot fool the master who

has him step away till he can come correct.

years of stumbling ensue: binging, black outs,
waking up in filth, lost time, headaches,
brain fog. three years barely getting by:
a blur of community college, side jobs,
his disappointed dad, his brother gone
to the streets, then found in an abandoned
house, dead for days, unrecognizable.

jolted straight. crushed by guilt, recriminations,
flashbacks. Ernie finds AA. works his program.
shares his story. dumps his shit. hits the diner
after meetings, coffee and cross talk
among some budding friends. finds a home
group he can fit in. gets a sponsor. shows up.

along the way, he spots a pretty dark haired,
older woman. Russian. Jewish. a gal with lots
more time in. immigrant, single mom, estranged
from her peeps and the vodka soaked ethnic
partying in the northeast Philly diaspora.

Ernie steps to her too soon. she gently holds
him off till he can put in more work,
complete his inventory, make more amends.

Ernie is stung. a smacked ass. wounded.
sponsor scrapes him off the floor. talks
humility, powerlessness and patience. listens
to his venting all hours. talks him down.
over and again. Ernie surrenders. stays

small. shows up. day by day.

returns to pumping pecs and lats. goes
back to the sensei hat in hand. the old
man intuits this man/boy is clean if
far from sober. allows him back.

practices his forms. works on balance.
eventually: Rachael redux. smaller. tentative.
low key. gradually they grope their way
to something like relationship. awkward.
clumsy. inching their way. demons resurface:
recovering souls easily wounded. bruised
skin raw. tense. setbacks. near disasters.

Ernie and Rachael work it. not quite passionate.
a tad romantic. more than a little comforting.
so much less lonely. they muddle through.

Ernie comes to love her little girl. Rachael
sees his gruff affection, hard-nosed nurturance.
believes in it. trusts it to be true. trusts him
at his scarred core to be a decent man.

knows about his damage. her past mistakes.
decides he's worth the risk. believes they
have a shot. Ernie's already made up his mind.

never was his mess this good. Rachael makes
him borscht and brisket. it's a good restart.

even a beginning.

Charlie

In hospital, at the end.

slipping fast now.
vaguely notices
that elevator feeling
deep in his belly
and on the end
of his queasy dick.

brings an almost smirk
to his slackened jaw
he slides gratefully
underneath,
wife and sons
at his side.

Charlie feels
the chip go
from his
shoulder
right before he
lapses to where
noise and

voices are above
water but he hears them
from beneath.

lying on the bottom.
peeing in the pool.
couldn't give a fuck
if anyone notices.

no one does.
catheter.

the hustle
and the hassle
finished.
no more
recriminations.
no letting go.

just gone

beyond feeling or caring

or contact.
a darkening
twilight drift
away.

the past few years
a nightmare.

roller coaster diabetes

fueled by late night sweets.

now sweats.

the botched hernia repair:
the disastrous scalpel slip.
sepsis. the colostomy,
the humiliations,
the nights of fitful
sleep in the recliner.

slow motion
tumble.
from lowly
to abyss.

coulda, shoulda
been a contender.
never got out
of his own way.

no big deal

anyways.

nothing is.

anymore.
really.

the end comes
down to this.

which is
a great escape:

oblivion.

thanks be.

Bill

(How I Reached Bottom)

Till my late forties,
you name a Philly
street, I could tell you
the nearest taproom.

Never turned a drink down.
Always lookin to wet my whistle.

Blackout boozing and whoring…
old school fireman,
from back in the day I was.

Happy-go-lucky
most of the time,
but every once in a blue,
I'd get a mean drunk on.

One night in '79
I'm in this bar near K&A
I'm tyin' one on,
and god knows why,

I get nasty pissed
at this fella sittin
nexta me.
Smash this guy
upside his head
with a beer mug.
Two good shots.

Before he knows
what's coming,
he's on his way down.
Head bust open,
blood spurting.

I'm blind raging.
Lookin' to do
some more damage,

Already woozy,
I totter over
this poor bastard;
don't know what
possessed me.

I'm leaning in
to whack him again!

I see this gory
mess of a face!
gashed raw meat
… empty eyes!
Within a cunt hair

of killing that man.

And there's this heat
rushing up at me,
coming off the blood,
and a strange metallic
smell in my nose,
and I fuckin just retch.

And right before I vomit
all over this guy,
they pull me off him.

In a cell 13 days
before the union lawyer
got me out...

still see that sad fucker's face.
still smell that hot sick smell.

That was the last drink I ever had.

Brian

(Thin skinned, bulging for trouble)

Inhabiting his business suit
like casing meant
for a smaller sausage,
thick necked Brian,
shaved head, ruddy
taut skin,
arrived looking
uncomfortably
dressed for
a special occasion.

Went about 260.
"roid" muscle.
Took my hand
in a vise grip lock
while searching
my eyes for something he
didn't seem able to find.

Held the look
till the glare thawed

into something
resembling a grin,
though it might
have been a smirk.

I smiled back,
feigning avuncular
Zen detachment:

"Do have a seat."

Thankfully he did.
And spilled his beans in
little uneven piles.

Former high school bully,
then body builder,
then construction worker.
Greased his hair trigger
with juice and
a king-of-the-hill
cockiness that beamed:
Do Not. Fuck. With Me.

Ascended rapidly
from laborer,
to torch man,
to knee breaker
in record time.

Favorite uncle
was the Union

president,
now doing time
for terroristic threats
and embezzlement.

With three other
officials
under indictment,
Brian now held
down the shop:
"Business Manager."
A pay grade
or two
over his head.

And now, he was
also a court referral.

Said it was bogus.
Did admit to scaring
the living shit out of his wife,
but swore she provoked him.

Talking about her fitness
instructor like he was some god.
Dared to look all disgusted
when Brian dropped in
for a surprise visit to the gym.
Found them talking
cozy after class.
Brian gripped her up,
then decked the trainer

for acting all concerned.
Poor bastard groveled and
refused to press charges,
earning Brian's
everlasting contempt.

The wife talked to advocates
in the courthouse.
Was keen to throw away his key.

He unloaded.
Enthusiastically
recounting
adventures
with the dipsticks
of this world.
Indignant,
vengeful glee
in crinkle-eyed smiles
illuminating
staccato
retellings of his
distribution of hurts
to so many deserving shits:
decking the huge
black dude in Target
for standing too close
at the check-out;
hanging a scab
off the roof
at a job site;
threatening

his daughter's
teacher for
asking personal
questions.

Now and then
his eyes drilled
in on me as if
looking for some kind
of connection.
Then I challenged
his right to snoop
on his "old lady",
Brian took sudden and
seething umbrage.

Had to surreptitiously
suck in a nervous breath
as he abruptly stood
to declare
his urge to throw me
out the window.

That laser stare flashed.

Then the grin/smirk.

My counter was a quivery
Buddha beam
followed by
an excruciating
pause.

I exhaled again only
after Brian turned heel
and sauntered
out the door,
leaving no indication
that this terminator
would be back.

Sean's Wife

Grateful Consolations

We'd only spoken
that one time
on the phone
during Sean's
evaluation, quite a while before.

Separated
since the arrest,
she'd been
hiding out,
petrified; a court order and a small baby.

With us,
he had been
chastened
and contrite.
"like a smacked ass" they say in Fishtown.

Sobered.
Unsteady.
Earnestly

on the
wagon. Squinting to see he'd broken his own heart.

Flailing at her
for hurts
suffered
way before he'd ever even met her.

Betrayed
by his own
wounded rage,
holding on
through crushing loneliness and shame,

He made appointments
prompt and regular;
looked to be trying hard,
till suddenly dropping out of sight, not returning calls.

Months went by before she rang
to tell me he'd
barricaded himself
in his flat, surrounded himself with empty vodka bottles,

Called her
weeping
to say goodbye.
Shot himself in the head still talking on the phone.

She whispered a teary
thank-you,
"If it wasn't for the program,

I'm sure he would have killed us both as well."

then we both wept
for twisted consolations.

Mona

Making the best of it

Mona was pretty in her own way.
mostly went unnoticed by guys
she tried to catch the eye of.
not too self-confident.
may not have been
the brightest bulb, but she had
a big heart, a kind soul, and folks
said she was good people.

light typing and answering
the phone at her uncle's warehouse
suited her just fine. had a crush
on one of the drivers who came by
bout once a week. Jeff didn't seem
to pay her much mind, but Mona
primped on days he might stop by.
dreamed he'd ask her on a date.

one day the hunk in question
pivoted on his way out the door.
one hand on the knob. stared at her

like he just had an idea. cool and
casual declared he and his buddy
had tickets to a neat show.
maybe she could join them.
mind blown, lightheaded, Mona said
sure, calm as she could muster.

spent several days on her outfit.
had to throw up a little in the office
toilet just before they picked her up.
they beeped. she ran out to find
a gal already sitting up front
with Jeff, so Mona jumped in back,
next to a shy looking dude who smiled
meekly. offered her a slug of Jack.

Joey had a plaid shirt on. said Squirrel
Nut Zippers was the act. she'd never
heard of them. had a few hits of weed.
a bit more bourbon. she did enjoy
the show. but even through the buzz,
booze and din, Mona was sad
to realize Jeff was, actually, with
the other gal, who did, in fact, seem
nice. Mona could see she was only
there to be the fix-up for his buddy.

they went for burgers afterwards.
drove to the river; parked, smoked
another jay, listened to some
tunes. things got blurry. soon
both pairs were messing round.

not really Mona's sort of thing,
but it had been a while since she
had even kissed. she slid into it.
glad for the attention. kinda
fun even though she wished
she could be up in front with Jeff.

Joey fumbled, fervent, maybe
nervous, maybe unfamiliar. but
gentle. careful. slow. Mona let
him open up her top. they were both
excited. it was weird, first time
and all, what with the lack of privacy,
(not that the other two paid any
mind). in the end, she was glad he
seemed so pleased, though it ended
faster than the action on the driver's
seat. Joey and Mona lay still, hugging
awkwardly till it went quiet up front.

super appreciative when they
dropped her off, Joey asked
for her number. wanted to see her
again. Mona said Ok
not to hurt his feelings.
called next day. interested. Mona
agreed. heart not quite there.

took her to an Italian restaurant.
just the two of them. wore nice slacks.
acted like a gentleman. they had the veal,
a little overcooked. the sauce

almost like her mom's. turned out,
he had a decent job at Sears.
played clarinet in a band.
sometimes got wedding gigs.
Mona was pleasantly surprised.
seemed so shy. hard to imagine
him on stage in front of people.

they had already had three dates,
no more sex after that first time
in the car, when she discovered
she was pregnant. Joe seemed
oddly pleased. Mona, near panic.
her parents a bit upset but also
a touch relieved: could have
turned out worse. at least he wasn't
Irish. seemed a steady enough guy.

they had a little saved up.
enough for a small wedding.
asked to set a date.
so fast for Mona. unsure.
pressured. diarrhea along with morning
sickness. felt a mess. finally decided
everything happens for a reason.
swallowed hard. hoped for the best.

looked great. make-up, nails,
special do. it rained the wedding
day. good luck, aunt declared.
no one mentioned her condition
to the priest. he didn't ask.

nice reception. Joey sat in on horn
after the main course. everybody
clapped. Atlantic City for the honeymoon.
just a long weekend. later that year
a little boy arrived. grueling labor.

but Mona managed pretty well. mom
was there when needed. helped her
with recipes. tips for breast
feeding and solid food. so finally
and all at once Mona had a family
of her own... not quite like the one
that she'd imagined. but maybe, if
she set her mind to being positive,
everything might just work out fine

Damon

fast and furious

Damon looked the part-time punk rock
drummer he was. cutoff shirts. sleeves
of ink. cycle chain bracelets. hair moussed
askew. sardonic snarl: persona carefully
assumed and outfitted. layered look,
assembled to allow quick off-stage
changes for his other gig: substitute UPS
driver, which made him enough for food
and rent for his basement flat below
a health food store on Passyunk, where
long and lean, he strode, shoulders
slouched, down the avenue.

as a kid, Damon was a holy terror.
child psychologist threw the book
at him: ADHD. Oppositional Defiant
Disorder. Dyslexia. god knows what
else. all agreed this boy was also
clever. which meant he could be wily.
a handful. always. inside his head,
a buzz of energy: impulses and

distractions. every desire an urgent
need. every emotion amped too high.
no control knob. no one at home
equipped to help him slow down.
contain urges. modulate frequency.
Damon was often frustrated. angry.

resentful of all efforts to regulate him.
yet needing exactly that. desperately. got
placed in e.d. class for slicing school bus
seats with his pen knife. loved it. found
untapped potential for himself among kids
with special needs. top of the misfit class.
freak BMOC. weirdly proud. cocky. had status.
bit of a top dog. smart mouthed teaser.
conjured vicious nicknames for the slow
and defenseless. in high school, Damon
morphed into a quasi-straight-edged rocker.

ate no meat. little dairy. no drugs stronger
than black coffee and vegan jelly donuts.
played drums in a band. practiced demonically.
crazy focus. dedicated to finding gigs.
sold his Adderall to girls in all-ages clubs.
earned a minor rep for retro tees, rad sneakers,
and a mad LP collection. covered his arms
in wild-assed tats. wiry. tough. no one
to mess with. could cop an attitude if
provoked. hard to predict. edgy. evacuated
home after graduation. never looked back.
made the scene on South Street. a regular
at Zipperhead and Lorenzo Pizza.

aspired to be a minor player, but Damon's
love life was opportunistic at best. episodic
at worst. mostly groupie types. lots of magenta
and Run Lola Run red hair. many embarrassingly
young. having slim game, he kept it light but
hyperactively intense. rarely swam in the deep
end. did not have the right stroke. fucked like
a punk drummer: hard and heavy from the
jump. quick strong finish. no downtempo. few,
if any, subtleties. the gals did not complain.
but most weren't round long enough to get

a chance to. during a particularly dry spell,
Damon started talking to a waitress at a local
restaurant. got his head turned round.
three-sixty. sweet dark-haired gal; Temple
college student, just washed up on the rocks
from a shipwrecked relationship. predilection
for bad boys. Damon saw his chance to snag
her on the rebound. pounced. extravagant
with promises. vows of deep commitment.
proclamations of true love. mouth writing
checks his ass could not cash. maybe conned
himself as well. clueless to his own ignorance.
shallow as the average puddle. shiny as an oil
slick on top. caught up in his own reflections.
dropping lines from old soul songs. lured
her in to share his underground pad. made
space (with mild resentment) for her belongings.

the honeymoon was passionate. but short lived.

Damon soon felt crowded and confused. her
clutter in his mess overwhelmed him. hard time
sharing space. time. belongings. tangled in moods.
fits of pique. no chops to play it out. began
to lose it over little things. started to yell. argue.
explode. then bailed abruptly. called it all off.
kicked dream girl to the curb. leaving his
waitress with the check. and handfuls
of crumpled tissues. seduced and abandoned.

and crushed. the breakup did not go well
for Damon either. fell into a pit. felt like
a shit. also missed the hell out of her.
empty. lonely. longing… remorse. went back
to her. begged forgiveness, wool cap in hand.
apologized. pleaded. got repeatedly denied. no
promises, no confessions, nor contritions could
woo her back. just told him to get help.

which, surprisingly, he did. deflated and
desperate, Damon called around. found
a guy who people said was good with hard
cases. fair, no nonsense, knew his way around
the block. reasonably priced. a therapist with
some edge. older but hip. shabby office vibe.
carefully direct. empathic. thorough. straight
shooter. drew him out. earned trust.

gathered history. got the picture. bided time.
once they grew tight, hit Damon between
the eyes: laid on hard realities; obvious
truths: Damon was his own worst enemy.

victim and perp of his own sad story. brain
chemistry a mess. attitude fairly shit.
rebel against no cause, except himself.
unwilling to contain or be contained.

same busy-brained, short fused boy.
tall toddler. tantrum ready to happen.
unsafe to hang around. intimately
dangerous. brain chemistry not his fault.
but his, and only his, responsibility.
job one. or else. all his shit forever
on a loop. reoccurring nightmare:

Damon resisted fiercely. walked out
in a huff. stung in recognition even
as he fled. petulant. defiant. brain
racing. all up in his head. eating
at him. murmuring. debating. replaying
arguments with the shrink, himself.
wanting to prove the therapist wrong.
doubting that even a possibility. took
his buzzing brain to his drum kit. beat
the piss out of the skins. found a handful
of groupie girls to pound as well.

therapist saw best odds in the long game.
left the door ajar, Damon chose to make his
play short-handed. missing the cards to even
ante in. left him a loser. from the jump.
which, in his heart, he knew he was.
crashed and burned several times. forced
himself to go back. showed up humiliated.

with guidance from a gentler hand, downshifted

into humble. got some traction. admitted
overwhelm. conceded he was not able
on his own. needed a mentor. a map.
needed to surrender. standing in a hole
too deep to see much of an horizon,
Damon was scared. lost. the shrink was
gentle. firm. they both knew it would
be hard. it would take time. it was. it did.

Craig

(the stripper's name was Summer)

she split wide
in the glaring
misty spotlight.

blonde heat,
rushing sap,
emerging buds:

this gentleman
at the club
was drenched
in Summer's storm.

infatuated.
besotted.
obsessed.

everywhere
became the street
where she lived.

blooms burst,
heat shimmered
off the steamy
tarmac.

He was transported
down the shore
where love songs blared
on the boardwalk.
And under it,
Craig tugged
at fantasies.
erecting a house
of pornographic
playing cards
out of hot thick,
humid air.

utterly beguiled,
Rabinowitz
conned himself
into believing
she would always
be his private dancer.

his Summer romance
became his endless love,
became the Ponzi scheme of borrowed cash,
became the insurance jackpot,
became the plot,
became the bathtub fiasco,
became the sordid tabloid banner.

became the endless sentence.

Now, locked down
inside his own imagination,
he whiles away a lifetime
of impossible daydreams:

a very unique,
very idiosyncratic,
seasonal affective disorder.

* The Craig Rabinowitz case was a major news story in the
affluent suburbs of Philadelphia in 1997. Craig was convicted of
murdering his wife and staging the scene to make it appear she had
drowned in the bathtub. During the trial it was revealed that
Rabinowitz was a devotee of strip joints in Philly where he had
spent extravagant amounts of money borrowed from friends and
family to shore up his failing medical supply business. He had
hoped to cash in on a life insurance policy to elope with the dancer,
stage named, Summer.

Ramond

One trial learning

Raymond lived life in reserve.
shy, quiet type, even as a boy.
exceptionally smart. remarkably
diffident. even when tiny. they
called him slow to warm up.
he was an only. dad a big deal
accountant. Big Four. mom
an officer at the bank. Citizens.
he had a nanny. went to an academy.
Chestnut Hill. father sharp of
tongue. sarcastic. critical.
mother, preoccupied but warm.
the nanny was the hugger.

never hit. occasionally scolded.
acquired thin skin, or always had
it. hard to tell. but the safest way
he kept himself, at home or
in school, was at a distance.
got teased a fair amount. avoided
it. head down. off. away. teachers

loved him. brightest kid in every
class. best grades. thuggish preppies
let him slide for copied homework,
glimpses of his tests. read the room.
got by. knew his spots.

never physically disciplined. never
had one fight. not in high school.
certainly not in college. aced it all.
Phi Beta Kappa. went to med
school. high honors. matched with
his top choice. chief resident. still
shy. still reserved. caught the eye
of an aspiring nurse. culled him
from the herd. joined him
in the corner. played the long game.
won him over. first squeeze for him
outside of set-up prom dates.
the sex, intoxicating. sealed his deal.
got married and signed on at his final
hospital placement. she held in her
stomach and her bile throughout
the courtship. let her breath and
criticism out after the Cancun
honeymoon. not since his daddy's
carping had Raymond heard so
much complaining. newlywed wife
swarmed. droned on. hovered.

tried to withdraw. she pursued.
stayed longer at work. she pounced
on his return. late one night she

drove him hard. felt cornered.
trapped. his recoil surprised him
too. lashed out. desperate. random
swing. caught her clean across
the face. in total shock she shut
up. in the stunned silence former
lowly mouse-spouse felt a powerful
surge. double barreled reinforcement:
her silence: relief. top dog exhilaration:
total high. straight to the head
of Pavlov's dog. instant one trial
learning. within a month he'd swung
three times more. silence and the power
rush on each occasion. then one disastrous
night, the reckoning arrived. in a tussle,
yanked her arm clean out of her shoulder
socket. ER visit. weak excuses. wide eyes.
veiled recriminations. flashed montages:
fearsome consequences. loss of license
and career. divorce court humiliations.
a life of exile not retreat. took a leave
of absence. sought out help. not proud.
not defensive. desperate. ashamed.

afraid of what he had become so
quickly. sad and sorry. mortified. not so
afraid to lose his wife. terrified to lose
his life: his career as he had pictured it.
she, too much. he, too ill-prepared. unready.
needed so much basic training. to learn
those things he'd missed while lurking
on the edges staying safe.

Colin

understudy at the last resort

I

stumbling out of stale chilled Greyhound air
into clouds of blue exhaust, Colin is broken
field high-stepping on the terminal sidewalk
round assorted hustlers and perverts, hauling
his duffle, gathering his bearings, avoiding eye
contact as much as possible. a tatty Mercedes
veers screeching to the curb. salt-and-pepper
bushy eyebrowed dude with an Adolphe Menjou
mustache rolls down the window and asks
in a heavy accent if he's looking for work.
Colin is fresh out from a Jersey boardwalk
job humping fries and snow cones. wages lost
to underaged beer and skank weed. no clue
what comes next. he's open to suggestions.

Colin's from Philly. not sure it's still home.
mom gone a few years. dad slowly drowning
in Yuengling. the "work?": dishwashing. hotel
kitchen up the mountains. a chance to learn
skills. move up to the prep line. the opening

is now if he's game. the kid shrugs. could be
a plan. jumps in. they wend their way up north.

II

a grand rambling wood shamble of a building
on a limpid lake in Sullivan County. glory mostly
faded from the gilded days of monied WASPS
who rode the now defunct rail line for lodgings,
gin and mountain air. last resort standing
for crusty knickered golfers, tweedy
day hikers, heel worn birders and cross
country skiers with wax-able wooden
runners. guest list padded now by hordes
of workaday proles looking to try
the toboggan run/water slide they read
about in the Sunday Travel Section. new
crowd less discerning, more easily impressed.
keeps the hotel from its foregone fate years
beyond the wrecking ball's estimated arrival time.

III

Colin falls madly ass-over-heels for the spacious
old world lobby dimly illuminated by Victorian
mahogany floor lamps, flapper frills for shades,
and the immaculate kitchen run by the Prussian
autocrat still acting as if his stage is set
in the Central Alps. Gustav assigns Colin a monk
cell in the staff dorm amidst a motley crew
of misfits handpicked from outer margins
by this culinary Fagen with an eye for outcasts

in transition from not much to no place better

IV

six years slaving in the galley, Colin slowly climbs
the line. head on a swivel, eyes and ears alert
to when to duck and when to hustle. holds his own
in gale force tirades. stands tall against withering
criticism. becomes the loyal opposition. wins
the despot's admiration for sheer determination
and ballsiness. makes a home among the shifting
band of nomads. earns respect. sets example.
becomes the old head role model practicing
each new station in off hours. sponging up details.
his "yes chef" always respectful. never kiss ass.

V

Gustav was as apt to throw a plate as to invite
a chosen few for champagne sipped with steak
tartare to celebrate some gastronomic triumph
or just because his mood is gusting from a milder
direction. patrolled his kitchen like a cock
in full prance, chef's hat bobbing, waitstaff
girls quaking in his wake. stung by rebuke.
puddles of tears. or gratefully relieved
to be graced with one of Chef's soft pinches
or light butt slaps. most endured casual
molestations as fine print on unread job
descriptions or, in the case of sadder souls,
as added compensation for jobs well done.
a select few were rumored to engage

in occasional after hours bendings over
butcher block for Chef Gustav. though
no one talked very much about such things.

VI

Colin studied everything the old man did
from sauté flair to the master's whimsy
with garnishes. mimicked knife techniques, even
his odd setup of the mis-en-place. learned
preps, sauces, soufflés, and the grill:
every station of the cross en route to sous
chef Calvary. with the number two position
came challenge, privilege, and the power
to piss downhill. which Colin used judiciously.

just bullying the most deserving. Colin left
the defenseless and pathetic for the despot's
toying. landing on only those from whom he
rightfully expected more. but license to hit
on servers was an entitlement Colin could not
allow himself to resist. early on he let the action
come to him. only moved on those who offered
themselves up for taking. later, tired of easy
marks, he practiced prepping, grooming, and
closing in on new hires like he did rehearsing
with the torch on creme brûlées: smooth
delicate passes repeated till deftness
was perfected. new girl Annie would have none

of the above. unsure but diligent; diffident but
strong willed; had a secret resume of survival

skills. learned them in a nightmare home where
she apprenticed under older sisters in defense
against unwelcome hands and drunken visitations.
her aloofness made her all the more attractive
to besotted Colin who dreamed about her alone

in his cell. Annie avoided Gustav's barbs and Colin's
come ons with a practiced knack for vigilant prediction.
quick feet. and a face that rarely let on what was
happening beneath. wouldn't cave to Colin's charm
or brighten to his twinkle. never allowed herself even
close to being left alone with the lecher-in-chief.

in the end the old man couldn't bear her cold
insouciance. took personal affront to Annie's
edgy self reserve while other servers trembled
in his presence. set out to break her down.
make her heel to his dominion. Colin saw
Gustav's next play coming. knew what humiliation
would ensue. could not bear to watch his apple
crushed. knew to challenge Chef was risky. yet he
stepped in just in time. stood Gustav down in front
of everybody. held his own throughout an epic clash.
earned props from the entire staff. finally captured
Annie's heart before they both were banished.

Vll

so the pair became a couple on the way back down
to Philly. found refuge on some friendly floors. picked
up restaurant gigs with ease because they knew
the ropes and were trained to do things properly.

Colin worked grill shifts, taking doubles when he
could. Annie found a smart cafe to earn good tips.
got themselves a tiny place. a tv and a bed. slowly
filled their flat with bargains from the thrifts.

at first Annie gave herself to Colin with a passion
born of gratitude. and of respect for his big heart,
hard-work ethic, and his sheer force of will.
she conceded he was cute but had to unlearn
her distaste for all that flirty stuff that fouled
her first impressions. never had a boyfriend
up till then, so shacking up with Colin was
a heavy dose of all at once. selecting furniture
and decorating great fun. eating his delicious
meals a special bonus. in bed she felt uneasy
past the first encounters. her history left her
queasy about what she was allowed to like
and do. or even feel. Colin had only ever had

short flings. practiced in the art of smooth talk
from his Seaside Heights nights, but beyond
charming come-ons, still a novice. clueless
about being clueless about pleasing women.
fairly good at getting gals to yes. not much
practice past scoring. apprenticeship under
Gustav may have honed his kitchen chops but
foreplay and intimacy skills were sadly lacking.

nights with Annie were Christmas in July. 365.
the gifts all had his name on them. Colin: quickie
sex, an expected reward for a hard night's work.
Annie: a routine drill to help get Colin off. fervent

humping. aromas of charred meat. groans. spastic
climax. a refrain of postcoital snoring. irksome,
yes, gradually growing into more than a minor
irritation to be sure, but nagging annoyance took
an immediate backseat to far more dramatic concerns
the day Annie realized she was pregnant.

VIII

both were stunned. both panicked. each prepared
their own escape. motherless children. from bruised
and broken homes. wanting so much more. and so
much better. neither sure what to do, or or how to act.
Colin, slapped by alternating waves: feeling trapped.
feeling guilty. Annie, accusing herself of foolishness
and stupidity. both wanting to be responsible. grown up.
both determined to make a better life than those who
raised them. in the end, they clung desperately
to each other. exhaled. hugged. decided to get married.

busied themselves with enjoyable distractions.
threw themselves into wedding plans. coordinated
potluck add-ons for Colin's planned reception spread.

IX

Annie didn't show much through the full cut dress
at the service. a grove in Fairmont Park. small buffet.
a few friends. restaurant pals. a mixed tape. a few
nice presents. a weekend honeymoon. Atlantic City.
the Claridge. all diverting. preoccupying. all temporary.
soon the evidence could not be ignored. anxieties

expanded to quiet terrors until a miraculous month four
transported Annie to amazing state of graceful fullness.

X

she bought books to familiarize herself with
what lay ahead. cajoled him to classes between
shifts. swelled. grew confident. sure footed.
he stood awestruck. intimidated as her belly
rounded and with it came a bloom of well being.

Colin felt distanced by the bulge. outside
the miracle happening within. her surging
self-containment recalled the from-the-mountains-
Annie. no pining now. just a growing odd bitterness.
he felt powerless. excluded. even the sex felt wrong.
perhaps because she seemed much more enthused.
he hung round after work schmoozing with the crew.
started sharing spliffs with bus boys round back.

when Annie didn't at first complain how late he
was getting in, he joined forays to after-hours
clubs to dance and booze with other restaurant
revelers. threw himself into the haze and sweat
and thumping music. staggered home fried and
frayed to catch a few winks before the rollercoaster
climbed again. soon with little insulation on his wires
he began to burn hot. short circuit. caught himself
insulting a dish washer with cruel invective he once
heard Gustav scream. at home he looked in horror
at his reflection in the bathroom mirror contorted
in contempt as Annie called him from another room.

due date looming, he was awash in doubt. exhaustion.

XI

Annie was worried about the late nights,
the drinking and the weed. could hear a shrillness
in her own voice. retreated into feathering the nest.
arranging piles of baby clothes. even with his hair-shirt
of resentments Colin couldn't justify his ornery ways.
drank and smoked more weed to dull the shame.

one night, at closing time, a needy well stacked
waitress asked Colin if he was going partying
that evening. flashed a vial of coke. winked
flirtatiously. he gripped her up. kissed her hard.
flipped her round. bent her face down over
the prep counter. pulled down her pants.
in a flash was transported to the hotel kitchen
back up the mountains. watching from a dark
corner. appalled. Chef Gustav was penetrating
a scared server from behind. Colin could see her
frightened face from the side. Gustav could not.
back at the restaurant, Colin pulled up short.
a wave of fear, shock, and disgust flooded over him.
Colin stopped abruptly. took a deep breath. exhaled.
patted the waitress softly on her ass. turned heel.

XII

wandered out of the kitchen. strode slowly home.
brain abuzz. rehearsing self recriminations, apologies,
confessions. found the chain lock on. a note scotch

taped to the door. "GET HELP" it read. he was ass smacked. stunned. rage surged instantly inside him. dissipated just as quickly. Colin expelled a resigned sigh. pivoted. slipped silently down the stairs. promising himself and Annie to come back correctly. knowing that he could. pledging that he would. realizing, finally,

he had some serious growing up to do. and, knowing, at last, he needed to find himself a new mentor.

Special Thanks

Special Thanks

I'd like to thank some dear friends for their assistance in the finalization of this book and its cover presentation. I have deep appreciation to my initial readers who provided valuable feedback and support for this project. Bill Van Buskirk, Anne Schneller, Dan Aharon, Stanley Yoder, Stephen Laruccia, Rob Carter, Natasha Watson, and Karl Stark were all extremely helpful with encouragement, guidance and critical reactions to early versions. Anne Schneller also proof-read and copyedited my early dyslexic drafts with patience and kind forbearance. Thanks also to Jody Cohen for her photography on the back cover.

Appreciation is also due my extended family of friends who have responded so positively over the years and urged me to collect my "mosaics" and publish an edited and expanded anthology of the characters and tales I have episodically presented to them. A few require singling out for their ongoing appreciation and encouragement: the late Irene Basil, Jerry Lindauer, Dennis Masella, Lawrence Jackson, Chris Hawkins, Patti Handle Barnes, Richard Courage, Robert Tierney, Julian Babcock, Jim Francis, Pat Desmond Vargo, Rachael Dash, Susan McLeer, Michael King, Jeanette Wilkins, Eileen Devlin, Barbara Hoepp, Robin Bott, Joan McKesson, Jim Dunn,

Rick Davison, Pricilla Kayes, Stephanie Kitchen, Rachael Nicole, Vern Lindauer, Georgette Bartell, Brooke Bankes-Polk, Mary Hale Meyer, Vernon Lee, Deborah Culhane, Phyllis Jacobs, Barbara Gilin, Robert Quinn-O'Connor, the late Barbara Bloom, the late Nate Passen, and the late David Dan.

Thanks, also to Gloria Detweiler, my dear wife, who gave me (as always) the space, time, support, and permission to pursue this project.